K

Inventions

by Oscar Cadejo
illustrated by Cary Pilo

HOUGHTON MIFFLIN HARCOURT
School Publishers

Printed in China

ISBN-13: 978-0-547-02167-6
ISBN-10: 0-547-02167-4

10 11 12 0940 18 17 16 15 14 13
4500443494

I love to invent things. I'm good at it, too.

In first grade, I had a great idea. I was using too much paper to do my homework. So I took a piece of notebook paper to the art store. They coated the paper with plastic.

I wanted to use the paper more than once, so I bought a marker that would easily wash off. Then I did my math homework on the plastic paper.

As I wrote, my dog Oscar watched me. But I should have remembered to watch him!

The next day I took my homework to school. When I handed it in to the teacher, he stared at the blank page. Oscar had licked all the numbers off the page!

Since then, I have invented many things. However, my inventions are not always successful.

One time my mother complained about Oscar's hair. Hair was on the couch, on the floor, and in the bed. She said, "If only that dog wouldn't shed!"

I had a great idea. I took an ordinary plastic bag and went to work. I cut the bag in the shape of a dog's body. I put the plastic suit on the dog, and he seemed to like it.

Then Ocar began acting strangely. He ran out the door and started barking. He scared the cat, and she fell out of a tree.

After that, Oscar went totally out of control. He ran back into the house and tore his plastic suit on the doorknob. He knocked over a lamp and my mother's fancy plates.

That invention was a disaster.

But the disaster gave me an idea. I thought, "If only things would not fall off tables!"

Meanwhile, my mother was upset. She said, "Did you see Fluffy fall out of the tree? What if that poor cat hurt herself?"

"It would take a lot of training to keep Fluffy out of the tree. Maybe we should keep the cat inside," my dad said.

Mom replied, "No! Fluffy enjoys the outside. I just wish she could fly like a squirrel."

Mom's words gave me another idea. With two good ideas, I had a lot of work to do. This invention had to be perfect!

First, I mixed modeling clay with glue. Then I glued the fancy plates and the lamp to the table. I nudged them with my hand, and they didn't move. SUCCESS!

I had more glue left. The bird cage might fall over, so I glued it to the table. I tried pushing it, but it would not move. SUCCESS AGAIN!

Then I began working on my second invention. I read three books on parachutes. Then I cut and sewed. Finally, my invention was complete. I had made a parachute for the cat!

I put the parachute on Fluffy. Then I told my parents, "I have two inventions that you will *love*!"

My mother eyed me suspiciously. I pointed out the window.

"Watch Fluffy!" I said.

The wind blew the parachute. Fluffy became confused and began running. The parachute opened and got very big.

To get away from the parachute, Fluffy ran up the tree.

Then Fluffy fell off the tree. As she fell, the parachute filled with air. Finally, she landed softly on the ground.

Fluffy ran inside the house. She hopped up on the table and then jumped onto the bird cage. The bird screeched, but the cage did not move.

My parents smiled. Mom said, "Look, Katy! Your inventions worked! The cat fell, but the parachute saved her. When she jumped on the cage, the glue held it on the table!"

I felt very proud. Finally, my parents said something good about my inventions.

The next morning my parents had something to tell me. I was worried. Maybe they wanted me to stop inventing things. That would be terrible! I loved inventing things!

"Katy," Dad said. "We know that you like to invent things."

I said, "But Dad!"

Dad held up his hand.

"Mom," I pleaded.

Dad continued, "So we think that you should go to a camp for inventors. For a month you can invent as much as you like."

I jumped up and down. I screamed and yelled. I hugged both my parents. I had no idea they could be so sensible!

"Thank you, thank you, thank you!"

The bird got excited, too. She started screeching. That scared Fluffy, who jumped on Oscar. The dog jumped up on the table. You'll never guess what happened next.

The lamp stayed on the table!

My parents smiled. So did I!

It was almost time for supper. Mom said, "What will I make tonight? Oh, if only I had a kitchen robot!"

I started to think. Then I started to think a little more. Hmm. What is the best way to make a robot?

Responding

TARGET SKILL **Story Structure** Who are the characters in the story? Where is the setting? What happens? Copy this chart and write your answers.

Characters ?	**Setting** ?
What Happens Katy invents plastic suit for her dog. ?	

Write About It

Text to Text Write a response paragraph that tells about another inventor you've read about. What did the inventor make? How did the invention work?

TARGET VOCABULARY

cage	sensible
confused	suspiciously
control	training
ordinary	upset

EXPAND YOUR VOCABULARY

disaster	parachutes
invent	robot
inventions	

TARGET SKILL **Story Structure** Tell the setting, character, and plot in a story.

TARGET STRATEGY **Infer/Predict** Use clues to figure out more about story parts.

GENRE A **fantasy** is a story that could not happen in real life.